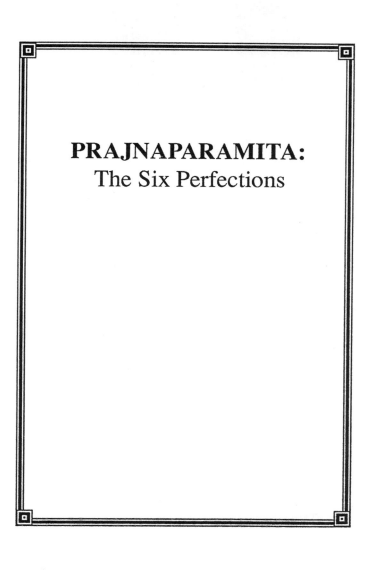

# PRAJNAPARAMITA:
## The Six Perfections

Copyright 1990
The Venerable Khenpo Palden Sherab Rinpoche
The Venerable Khenpo Tsewang Dongyal Rinpoche

Second Edition Printing 1991
Special Limited Edition, First Printing 1990

**Published by *Sky Dancer Press***
P.O. Box 1830
Boca Raton, Florida 33429

Sky Dancer Press Publishers:
      Executive Editor:  Joan Kaye, PhD.
      Design Editor:  Nancy Ash
      Business Management:  Sharon Raddock
      Special Consultant: Daniel J. Darcy, Esq.
      Marketing Consultant: William Hinman

**With many  thanks to Dharma Artist, Larry Peterson,
for his cover art, *Lotus Flower*.**

**Many thanks to Debi Harbin of Orlando, Florida for her
photographs on the back cover and pages 15, 18, 58 and 93.**

ISBN 1-880975-00-9

Printed in the U.S.A. by Dependable Printing, Miami, Florida

# PRAJNAPARAMITA:
## The Six Perfections

### Venerable Khenpo Palden Sherab Rinpoche

*Translated By*
**Venerable Khenpo Tsewang Dongyal Rinpoche**

*Edited By*
**Joan Kaye, Ph.D.**

*Design Editor*
**Nancy Ash**

*SKY DANCER PRESS*   *Highland Beach, Florida*

# A Biographical Sketch of The Venerable Khenpo Palden Sherab Rinpoche

The Venerable Khen Rinpoche is one of the most qualified scholars and teachers of the Tibetan Buddhist Tradition. He entered Gochen Monastery at the age of six, where he underwent an intensive training in all facets of Tibetan education, both secular and religious. In 1953 he graduated to Riwoche Monastery in Eastern Tibet, where he trained to become a Khenpo, or Professor, of Tibetan scholastic and philosophic studies. He fled to India in 1960.

Khenpo Palden Sherab has taught Buddhist philosophy and lectured on Tibetan culture while associated with faculties of India's most prestigious universities, notable among them the Sanskrit University of Benares where he has been head of the Nyingmapa Studies program for over eleven years.

Rinpoche came to the U.S. on a sabbatical leave in 1980 and has taught extensively throughout the United States, Canada and Europe.

Khenpo Palden is highly recognized for his profound understanding of the four schools of Tibetan Buddhism, his knowledge of the Tantras and as a meditation master. He is the author of several learned works and Tibetan language books. As a scholar of renown he has received many honours from His Holiness, the Dudjom Rinpoche and other leaders of the Tibetan people. Khenpo Palden Sherab, the Khen Rinpoche, is considered a Master of Dzog-Chen, the most highly developed and advanced tradition of spiritual practice pertaining to Tibetan Buddhism.

## A Biographical Sketch of The Venerable
## Khenpo Tsewang Dongyal Rinpoche

Khenpo Tsewang Dongyal has studied with many great Tibetan scholars and is a holder of the complete transmissions and initiations in the famous Kama and Terma Lineages of the Nyingmapa School.

Rinpoche is a graduate of Sanskrit University and has spent many years in Kathmandu at the Wishfulfilling Nyingmapa Institute teaching Buddhist Philosophy, Tibetan Culture and Poetry.

In 1978 he was invested with the authority of Khenpo (Abbot) by His Holiness Dudjom Rinpoche, and consequently presided at Orgyen Chokhorling Monastery. Today, Khenpo Tsewang is teaching Dharma in centers, colleges and universities throughout North America.

An active teacher and scholar, Khenpo Tsewang is also a published poet. He has also acted as translator for the Khen Rinpoche while the latter has been on tour visiting Universities and Study Centres in Europe, Canada and the United States. Khenpo Tsewang is a recognized expert in the study of ancient Tantric literature.

---

*Both the Venerable Khenpo Palden Sherab Rinpoche and the Venerable Khenpo Tsewang Dongyal Rinpoche are responsible for founding **The Sarnath Project**, in an effort to establish a college of traditional Tibetan education in India.*

Dedicated
to the Long Life
of

**Venerable Khenpo Palden Sherab Rinpoche**
and
**Venerable Khenpo Tsewang Dongyal Rinpoche**

*The Padmasambhava Buddhist Society*

# Dedication
*The End of Suffering*

The end of suffering was the Buddha's fundamental teaching. It is called the Four Noble Truths.

A "people" suffer too.

Individuals also suffer, but from the viewpoint of human psychohistory, one group of people has inflicted suffering on another group of people throughout historic time, and have themselves experienced suffering.

The approaching twenty-first century marks the end of a period and the beginning of an epoch where people cross borders and interact. Civilization historically experiences an enrichment. In the West, for example, American democratic innovative spirit brings a paradigm shift of enormous complexity. The interaction and interconnection between migrating people shift cultural patterns in new and astonishing ways. Old barriers of archaic notions and embedded misconceptions break down when one no longer sees just the stereotype. One experiences the person, the essence. One faces the other, the I - and - the- other become the I - and - the - Thou. That distinction breaks down too, and perception becomes nondual. A unitive sense pervades. Dzog Chen, a Nyingma Tibetan Buddhist teaching, roughly translated as "The Great Completion" relates this experience as "the pure natural".

Out of this diversity rich exchanges occur. Cultural membranes are permeable, like everything else, and a new complexity arises in the self-correction. The human yearning for quality change is a built-in attribute of individuation. We just need to relax and "unpack", get comfortable and happy, be both earthy and spiritual.

Human suffering is worldwide six oclock news, regularly reported to millions of viewers simultaneously through mass media. Complexity and crisis within a planetary electronic neural network has produced an information age. Infiltrating exchanges percolate through the environment. A new awareness has produced the space age. We are all maturing. Whether we are evolutionarily aware is another topic. Nature dictates and we adapt. Unless we realize this ultimate biophysical and planetary fact, we all, a humanoid earthform living amongst other earth forms, suffer.

The Nobel Peace Prize was given to the spiritual leader of Tibet -- His Holiness, the Dalai Lama, for his stand on nonviolence. Mindfulness and nonviolence are basic Buddhism. The powers of envisioning are not limited to the powers of vision, and His Holiness, the Dalai Lama's vision is a knowing about peace that includes but transcends the politics of peace. He received the award for highlighting the need for an end to suffering and a new vision of what it means to be a peaceful free human in a possible society.

A "people" need to be kind to each other. Down through long passages of historic time, the family of nations have not been known to treat each other in compassion and spiritual nobility.

The Four Noble Truths (whose focus of subject matter is the end of suffering) is the Buddha's foundational teaching. In a time calling for planetary healing on all eco-logical levels, we feel indeed fortunate to be able to share the richness of teaching given by two Buddhas in this fortunate eon.

Khenpo Palden Sherab Rinpoche (meaning Glorious Wisdom, Precious Jewel) and Khenpo Tsewang Dongyal Rinpoche (meaning Life Empowerment, Precious Jewel), bring to Florida direct transmission teachings from the most ancient lineage of Tibet (The Nyingma Lineage). May the rich treasures of humanity be preserved for the enlightenment and nonsuffering for all sentient beings.

Joan Kaye, Ph.D.

# Contents

**PART THREE**
*The Mind of Enlightenment*

ཡ་ར་ར་ཡ་ཤགས་ར་ར་ཤི་མི།་ར་ཡ་ར་ར་ར་ར་ར་ར་ར་ར་ར་ར་ར་ར་ར།

VEN. KHENPO PALDEN SHERAB RINPOCHE

I would like to thank all those who helped bring these Prajnaparamita teachings into print, especially Joan Kaye, who meticulously transcribed and edited the text. The version presented here is a faithful rendering of the Prajnaparamita as I taught it and as it has been transmitted from Buddha Shakyamuni in an unbroken lineage of great masters. May these teachings pervade the ten directions for the unceasing benefit of sentient beings in all six realms!

SARVA MANGHALAM

Ven. Khenpo Palden Sherab Rinpoche

# *Introduction*

In July 1989 two Tibetan Nyingma Buddhist Lamas, the brothers, the Venerable Khenpo Palden Sherab Rinpoche and the Venerable Khenpo Tsewang Dongyal Rinpoche gave teachings to the Padmasambhava Society in Miami, Palm Beach and Orlando, Florida concerning the mind of enlightenment.

Khenpo Palden Sherab Rinpoche began the first of eight teachings with the renowned spiritual treasure, the Prajnaparamita. Khenpo Palden spoke with a natural ease and depth stemming out of his understanding and experience of the Prajnaparamita and the Six Perfections; the means to enlightenment through an evolution of consciousness.

Spoken with simple clarity and quiet joy, these ancient teachings are universal, dynamic and current for our swift time. Khenpo Palden explains the skillful means for the end of suffering, the meaning of being human, and the holomovement towards optimal ecological planetary well being. Buddhism has always recognized the kinship of all living form.

Healing exists as a transformation process, as in the Six Perfections practice. Suffering can be experienced as a moving towards wellness, towards wholeness in a self-organizational model in self-correction evolving in conscious awareness. Mind has the capacity to store information in awareness towards spacious self-governance in compassion and emptiness bliss. This dynamic is an ongoing capacity of intelligence, refining and repatterning in greater creativity and success. Such felt joy is a learning to learn.

Khenpo Palden re-presents the teachings of the Six Perfections of Generosity, Self-Discipline, Tolerance or Patience, Joyful Effort, Concentration and Wisdom so simply and effectively that healing is implicit in the foundational compassion and loving-kindness. Rereading and reaffirming it again and again increases its clarity, like a jewel being repolished or a mantra resung. In this practical way, The Six Paramitas (Six Perfections) are a learning to learn and an awareness producing a global consciousness motivated by wellbeing.

In modes of compassion and loving-kindness the Six Perfections are an unlimited reaching out that is an expansion of consciousness, the consciousness state of the bodhisattva. This self-healing dynamic (autopoiesis) is a natural function of life. Khenpo Palden brings forward the knowing that life in-forms and in our joy, human embodiment is a precious gift. The unlimited is a boundless expansion. Through the practice of the Six Perfections comes the kinship with all living form through compassion. Like the unfolded lotus, the Six Paramitas expand us in an awareness of the perfection of wisdom that is called the Prajnaparamita.

In emptiness, the Prajnaparamita is the Transcendental Wisdom Knowledge. The Six Perfections or Paramitas are enfolded in the Prajnaparamita. The parts are in the whole. The whole, the Prajnaparamita, transcends the parts plus one because it is based on the truth of emptiness. The human unfolding expansion of compassion and loving-kindness in union and in unbounded expansion interpenetrates the ultimate enfolding contraction of emptiness and no self. This budding is the bodhisattva knowing of compassion and emptiness for the sake of all sentient beings and is a spheroid knowing.

The Six Perfections are a Skillful Means practice for our ordinary everyday interactions with each other. We are each other's flower. The Absolute Prajnaparamita, the wisdom transcendental knowledge is the birthing mother of all the buddhas, based upon emptiness (sunyata) and the total extinction of all self-interest.

The Venerable Khenpo Palden Sherab Rinpoche and the Venerable Tsewang Donygal Rinpoche bring to their teachings living qualities that can only be hinted at: evolved, joyful, friendly, dignified, balanced, are some of their qualities that spring to mind. It becomes increasingly evident that the Rinpoches and their teachings are inseparable.

**Joan Kaye, PhD.**

# PART ONE

## Prajnaparamita:
## *Supreme Wisdom Knowledge*

# 1 Prajnaparamita: Supreme Wisdom Knowledge

## The Meaning of the Word Prajnaparamita

Prajnaparamita is one Sanskrit word, made up of two words: Prajna and Paramita. When we understand the two Sanskrit words, we intuit meaning.

The first word, Prajna, has two syllables—Pra and Jna, and each syllable is special. Pra, the first syllable, has many different connotations such as supreme, first or unique. Jna, the second syllable, means knowledge, wisdom, understanding, realization. The two syllables coming together in one word, Prajna, mean: supreme knowledge, unique realization, transcendent knowledge.

## Supreme Knowledge,
## Unique Realization,
## Transcendent Knowledge

The second word, Paramita, has four syllables. One could say, *"crossed over"*, or *"gone over to the other shore"*. The Sanskrit word, Paramita, then means a *"leading beyond"* mundane knowing to a transcendent knowing. The realization and the practice coming out of this knowledge leads us beyond to a higher state of consciousness called nirvana or the buddha state.

Prajnaparamita is transcendent wisdom. We all know that there are innumerable subjects to learn. Prajnaparamita is unique because it leads beyond subject matter, yet includes it. A priority of knowing is established as the ground state of awareness, and the outcome of this knowledge leads us to the enlightenment state. This is why it is called the ultimate or supreme knowledge.

Our everyday world is completely mingled with our emotions, with thoughts and with contradictions. Prajnaparamita frees us from obscurations, clinging and duality thought. Prajnaparamita takes us beyond these duality states of consciousness to an overarching knowing.

## Three Ways of Understanding Prajnaparamita

How can we understand Prajnaparamita? According to Buddhist philosophy, the view or basic ground state is the first understanding. Continuation Activities are the second. The Result follows. In this continuum are the three modes of understanding Prajnaparamita.

For example, the basic ground state "IS" the view. The basics are the foundation of the practice of the six perfections. Without a good beginning, the rest doesn't follow. It is the state of mind that matters.

This basic ground view isn't hidden from us. Our situations and our perceptions reveal our basic consciousness state in everyday events and phenomena, as our very own experience. Direct introduction, continuation and the result reveal the Prajnaparamita as direct experience.

We can, by way of logical explanation, summarize this process into two parts or five parts. The division into five parts are the categories Buddhism calls aggregates. The five aggregates are form, feeling, perception, formation and consciousness. The two categories are subject and object. This division into two, subject and object, is called duality thinking. We are able to see many different things, but for all the diversity, there are only two categories—subject and object.

This basic ground view
isn't hidden from us.  Our situations and our
perceptions reveal our basic consciousness state
in everyday events and phenomena, as our very
own experience.

## The Stages

The Prajnaparamita is like the clear light.   Like
sunlight, it dispels the darkness of ignorance.

Buddhism defines ignorance as not knowing mind's
nature. In ignorance the natural clarity of mind is obscured
by negative emotions. These obscurations develop in the
duality state.

Duality is very strong, whether we perceive the
world through the focus of subject and object, or through
the view of the five aggregates of form, feeling, perception, formation and consciousness. Our own ego demands
a subject-object separation. Duality is  strong, solid,
real, and permanent; therefore we cling strongly. This is
the first stage.

As soon as we develop attachment, the "I" is created.
"I" senses the  other, the  "object".  This is the second

stage.

The third development, the "my" or "mine" of personal belonging produces greater clinging. The dual states of attachment and rejection co-exist and the preciousness of oneself naturally arises. No one has to teach us this. Spontaneously it arises. One's own self is considered to be more important.

These three stages of ego in Buddhism begin with the subject (where there is more attachment to oneself) and the belief in our separability, then the natural arising of the object, and finally the clinging to "mine", with its subsequent rejection of the other. Distance from the other and hatred of the other is the root of all the confusion, delusion and ignorance. Our nests are then polluted.

Attachment brings thoughts of rejection, anger or hatred. Jealousy arises easily. Jealousy occurs when somebody you don't like experiences something better than you or attains some benefit or other that you would like. Emotions such as pride or arrogance can also arise if something good happens to us. All these emotions are called obscurations.

Where do all these emotions come from? They come from the ignorance state of not knowing mind's nature. Prajnaparamita, the supreme wisdom knowledge, dispels the darkness of ignorance like the sunlight.

> ### *The Prajnaparamita is like the clear light. Like sunlight, it dispels the darkness of ignorance.*

## Three Ways of Developing Prajnaparamita

Wisdom evolves in three different stages. The first phase is studying or listening. We hear the teachings. This basic ground state is called the view. The second stage is contemplation. We contemplate the teachings again and again. In the third phase we meditate and internalize what we have heard until it becomes the lived experience, an enfolding and unfolding yoga, or union of emptiness and wisdom. This yoga is a felt knowing, a certainty wisdom. Individuation is the opening of the various chakras, including the heart chakra and the wisdom eye; to see, think and intuit transcendence, and to act out of such knowing.

# 2  Relative and Absolute Reality

## Relative Reality

Prajnaparamita, the transcendental wisdom knowledge, is an understanding in two ways: in relative and absolute reality.

Relative reality contains multiple objects and many human beings. All of us have the same goal in that no one wants to be hated. No one wants to be unhappy. No one wants to be hurt. We all want joy. We all want to be appreciated by others. We each need good air to breathe, clean water to drink, as well as nutrients to sustain us. We want love and the benefits of compassion.

Each person's focus is on his or her own happiness and on his or her own peace and comfort level. Everyone's concentration is the same, and all sentient beings appreciate the value of kindness, love and compassion. Separateness creates boundaries. No special reasoning is needed to know this, and no logic is necessary for this understanding. Buddhism calls this popularly acknowledged and commonly understood experience, the relative reality.

## Absolute Reality

The spacious nature of emptiness is experienced in absolute reality. Mind is open, radiating and intelligent. Mind is a great emptiness. The quality of mind is that it reflects - - sparkling and radiating light in every direction. The nature of mind is clarity, clear light and luminosity for the nature of mind is already enlightened.

Relative reality considers this "I" or ego as very strong and solid. Where is this ego? When we say "I", most people are referring to their body. What do we mean by that? Is ego a part of our head? Is ego part of our neck, chin, arm, feet, belly or bones? We have 360 major bones according to Buddhist thought. Ego isn't in bones. Ego isn't a part of the body. Even if we lose a part of our body, we don't lose the ego. Ego remains. Through such reasoning we understand that ego isn't part of the body, and doesn't depend upon the body. Contemplating from gross to fine level we can't find ego.

Searching further to the finest state of matter, to the atomic structure, or even beyond that to the subparticle, the partless or the massless, ego can't be found. However much we search, we cannot find ego to be identical with the body in any way. If someone takes the far fetched notion (which people do not) and say, "the ego is something totally different from my body", that notion also is false. We don't take the view, "Oh maybe ego is on the table there, or somewhere else in my apartment". We don't believe that. We see that ego is neither different from our body nor part of it.

We can't find ego after such investigation. Yet as long as we believe in ego, confusions and chaotic situations arise and manifest, showing that ego is merely a concept, a way of thinking. As soon as we remove this notion, loving- kindness and pure compassion are immediate and available.

Awareness in emptiness is called absolute reality. We didn't find ego because there is nothing to find. Clinging and ego are the dualistic state. Investigation through logic brings us to this conclusion. Spacious awareness is a regressing back to source, beyond nirvana and samsara duality, like a child going into a mother's lap. Nirvana is a higher order of reality, spacious and spontaneously relaxed, and is unconditioned in that it is not made up of parts or duality. Components inhabit a whole.

After receiving this view concerning the basic ground state of egolessness or emptiness, examine your own wisdom. After the teaching, contemplate in a continuation activity practice. Buddha Shakyamuni said this, too. "You've received my teachings, now examine it for yourself, in your own wisdom."

---

**Look with your own wisdom.
Check it out yourself
rather than taking someone
else's word.
When you find that,
remain in that state.
Do not be confused.**

---

### Certainty Wisdom

Examine your own wisdom, till you find your own certainty wisdom. Otherwise an element of doubt may remain. The Buddha taught the inner way, the way of Certainty Wisdom. This is found in contemplation.

In Certainty Wisdom it is very important to remain in the true natural state which is an awareness of awareness that illuminates the meditator. Examine your own wisdom and mingle it with the Buddha's teaching for Certainty Wisdom.   You reach a wisdom far beyond mundane thought. This contemplation is very important.

*"Examine your own wisdom, till you find your own certainty wisdom.*

*Otherwise an element of doubt may remain.*

*The Buddha taught the inner way, the way of Certainty Wisdom. This is found in contemplation."*

## Doubt

We are beginning practitioners. We are ordinary human beings, and we have many obscurations and obstacles. One of the major obstacles is doubt or hesitation. It is a matter concerning mindset.

Doubt disturbs us, always makes trouble and prevents us from success. Doubt is quite natural and its source is ignorance. Doubt stays with us for a long time, according to the Buddha, but it disappears in the first stage of enlightenment, in Certainty Wisdom.

In Buddhism this first stage of enlightenment is called the first bhumi. There are ten bhumis or stages of realization. Doubt is common in human beings and is dispelled in the first bhumi, called the state of extreme joy. Enthusiasm as a state of consciousness is energetic. It is light and warm. Life is brighter with more possibilities. Options and pathways appear. The other interacts in pleasant ways; relationship by nature is reciprocal. Joy is contagious, enlivening and energizing the other. The other is attracted because vivacity is heightened and life feels fuller.

Conquering doubt is very important. Through contemplation we acquire Certainty Wisdom. Certainty means certainty about your view, your practice. For example, I can say "now I am sitting on this blue blanket"

(Khenpo Tsewang points to the blue blanket underneath him). Once I realize it is blue I have no doubt as to its color. I know it is not red or pink, or whatever. This confidence is self known in investigation and contemplation.

## Investigation and Contemplation

Investigation and contemplation are very important. Contemplate both subject and object. The subject, we have seen, is empty. Although we believe in the I, ego is nonexistent upon investigation.

The object also is empty. A house seems solid. By putting the name and the object together, we have the concept, "house". Without investigating the concept called house, people think the house is solid and nonseparable. Many different objects hold the "house" together. Examine this more carefully. House is a combination of billions of atoms as well as a combination of many objects. We know now that the subject or ego is nonexistent. But maybe we still feel things are solid, like this house.

The noun "house" is totally different. There are many objects and a combination of hundreds of things that make up the parts that we call house, such as wood, plastic, cement, windows, nails—many things. The name of house has no relationship to the many objects. Break down the concept of house, look at the separate objects and ask if they are the house. We will say, "this object (nail, perhaps) is not a house". "That object (window) is not a house". Investigate in this way; there is no house. House is an illusion. It is based totally upon the emptiness state. This is just an example. All objects are the same.

True investigation as Buddha taught shows the empty nature of reality. Everything is like a bubble, or reflection of the moon on the water. All dharmas should be regarded as dreams, the insubstantiality of thoughts with no position to uphold, like an illusion, a reflection in a mirror, a rainbow or mirage. Like an echo, contemplate the nature of unborn insight— rootless.

Careful observation in this way helps us remove dualism. Our present mind is developed in a contradictory way. High - low, big - small, dirty - clean, good - bad, we create judgments. If its big, it can't be small. If it's small, it can't be big. If it's dirty, it can't be clean. Developing in this way we cling to our notions. Mind struggles with those contradictions, which is itself mind.

## The "I" does not exist.

*One's own self makes mind smaller.*
*Relying on the true natural state,*
*we reach  beyond ego.*
*When mind realizes this emptiness state,*
*everything is completely equal.*
*This is called the Vastness State.*

All the complexities and ideas that are developed by one's own mind are not always true. What one person considers bad, another considers good. Good and bad do not exist in an external state, but in an internal state. In a spacious view the opposites are defined by their connection. For example, measure unites high and low. Judgment connects bad and good. The opposite holds the tension.

**There are many discussions
on emptiness in Buddhism.
Emptiness is not a blackness or darkness.
Emptiness is a fullness and openness.
Everything we see arising is
due to this emptiness.
If there were no emptiness, we could not see
change or development.
Emptiness is therefore the Openness State.**

# 3 Practice

*The basic view of the Prajnaparamita is the empty nature of subject and object. The continuation of this understanding is called Practice.*

Meditate and practice, and slowly, finally you will see this empty nature of reality all the time. Obscurations, anger, ignorance and jealousy leave, and loving-kindness, compassion and wisdom develop. You will perceive this entire universe like a reflection, like the moon on the water.

## The Third Wisdom Eye

As your practice continues, more and more of your inner natural state or inner wisdom is revealed. Your

wisdom will shine more brightly. Your capabilities will be greater, and you will be able to help others more. Wisdom spontaneously and naturally arises from the nature of mind. Buddhism calls this the Third Wisdom Eye knowing, which is capable of seeing far beyond the mundane view seen with these two bubble eyes.

Through the Third Wisdom Eye, the profound emptiness view of phenonema is realized. Maintain mind in Dharmakaya, the uncreated state and rest perfectly in the true nature state. Anywhere the mind goes there will still be the basic ground of Dharmakaya behind it. At this time you can also read past, future and present quite clearly.

Now it is beyond our capacity even to think of that state. Through the Third Wisdom Eye state, you will also be able to read the three times at one time. Everything becomes more ordered and apparent. Buddhism believes in past lives and future lives. In this consciousness state you will also know past and future lives, your own schedule, your own births and deaths.

At this time we don't know our past lives and future lives, not because they doesn't exist, but due to our ignorance concerning mind's nature. Ignorance is pervasive thoughout every direction from us. We know only what we see and experience at this moment. We do not see any other worlds nor do we know outside this moment. This emptiness or spaciousness is a subtle understanding known to those of great wisdom. By meditating upon emptiness in the state of complete tranquil abiding, the nothing-to-see will see that seeing.

## Continuation Activity

The continuum of our past and future lives is what is called Continuation Activity. Mind is continuous. Our present mind comes from the past lifetime or past mind. Our next lifetime arises from this present mind. Like other objects, such as a grain, tree, flower or fruit, the seed from the past grows in the future. Continuous, like a river, the past flows forward.

Those people who have the ability to know their births and deaths are known as bodhisattvas. These courageous beings have taken birth in this world in order to benefit sentient beings.

Prajnaparamita is the great emptiness. Emptiness is free from the duality, free from ego and clinging. This state is known as Prajnaparamita. To realize this state we meditate. Realization will not come through discussion or lecture, but through applying one's own mind. In Buddhism this is called meditation.

## *Prajnaparamita*

## *is the*

## *great*

## *emptiness*

# PART TWO

## *The Six Perfections (Paramitas)*

# 4 The Six Perfections (Paramitas)

## The Six Paramitas

The practice of Prajnaparamita is meditation. Meditation means maintaining the mind in its natural state. Without thoughts, leave the mind in the pure natural. Most of the time we do this as a sitting practice.

When we are not in sitting practice, or when we are out in the world, we can do other practices. They are called Paramita Practices. There are five paramitas or perfections you can practice in the world. The sixth paramita, Primordial Wisdom Transcendent Practice is called Prajnaparamita. There are six paramitas in all.

*Generosity*

Self-Discipline

Tolerance

Joyful Effort

**Concentration**

*Primordial Wisdom*

## The Six Paramitas are:

*1. Generosity Transcendental Practice*
*2. Self- Discipline Transcendental Practice*
*3. Tolerance Transcendental Practice*
*4. Joyful Effort Transcendental Practice*
*5. Concentration Transcendental Practice*
*6. Primordial Wisdom Transcendental Practice*

The first five perfections are most important. They must however, be combined with the sixth practice, the practice of Primordial Wisdom. The six paramitas benefit all sentient beings as well as oneself. The six perfections reveal enlightenment.

These practices are very special. Even if you practice just one of them for the first time, you will derive positive benefit. They are called Beneficial Practices, and are totally based on compassion, loving-kindness and wisdom. Attitude counts as the state of mind in which we find ourselves. Attitude colors our experience and directs action.

The six paramitas are the principle practices of a bodhisattva. All five paramitas combined with the sixth paramita are very powerful, removing our obscurations.

## 1. Generosity

The First Paramita is the perfection of generosity. When we are generous we give freely. Generosity removes the obscuration of miserliness. Miserliness is a form of clinging and attachment. The Paramita of Generosity creates nonattachment and helps others.

The Perfection of Generosity is the sense of self-existing openness and is based on making friends with yourself by discovering your own richness. Therefore, neither hold back, nor scheme your own project. Constantly give out. The consciousness that realizes that phenomena are not solid is the State of No Poverty. Giving out, opening up is a treasury of wealth.

## 2. Self-Discipline

Self- Discipline, the second perfection, is the opposite of wildness. This practice removes the wildness of our body, of our speech and of our mind. Self-discipline Transcendental Practice is morality and integrity. This antidote to wildness brings peace to ourselves and others.

## 3. Tolerance

The third paramita is the perfection of Tolerance, which removes anger and intolerance through patience. Anger disturbs others and ourselves. It is a matter concerning mindset and matter is mutable. Sick people, a sick society and a sick earth are interrelated levels of functioning. Loving-kindness and compassion heal.

## 4. Joyful Effort

Joyful Effort, the Fourth Perfection, removes the obstacle of laziness. Laziness is a big obscuration. Joyful Effort brings beneficial activities to ourselves and others.

## 5. Concentration

Concentration is the Fifth Perfection. The practice of Concentration will bring you the power to control your own mind. Control your own mind, and you release all the miserable feelings that come with the wildness mind.

Many people in this world are completely crazy. This happens because they cannot control their own mind. Many people also become upset or sad. This is a sign that they do not control their own minds. Also many thoughts and concepts keep our minds very busy. These are also signs that we do not have any power over our own minds.

Concentration will help to bring our minds into silence and into a peaceful state. At present our mind is very wild and very, very unstable. Concentration helps bring a state of calm and clarity. Concentration Practice will remove the wildness thoughts.

At this time it is most important for us to tame mind. Now, next time, tomorrow, next year, we become happier, more delightful, more peaceful with greater wisdom.

## 6. Transcendental Wisdom Practice

The Sixth Paramita, the Transcendental Wisdom Practice, I have already spoken about at length. Again briefly, when we develop this sixth perfection or paramita, we remove contradictions and obscurations, which are duality thoughts. The Transcendental Wisdom Paramita removes clinging which is due to dualistic mind. In this way we reach the ultimate, the Equanimity State.

These different paramitas can be done individually, each for a short time. You can meditate on one of the perfections. For example, if you do not feel ready to give forth greatly, you can meditate on generosity.

Gradually your capabilities will increase. Don't ignore your own gifts. Meditation and practice spontaneously bring the inner joy from within your own heart and mind. This joy is incomparable to any other joy, because it is revealed from the deep nature of mind. Its duration is long, creating benefits for yourself and other sentient beings.

These Six Perfections open your mind and your wisdom, and you will feel great joy all the time. The joy in your heart will bring joy to other sentient beings, because the Paramitas are totally based on loving-kindness and compassion. As I said before, this joy surpasses other joys. No other joys, like parties or picnics, bring the same qualitative benefit.

Practice in your daily life, in the office, in your home, wherever you are. Carrying the light, you are benefiting yourself as well as others. This is the Essence Practice of the Prajnaparamita, as well as the essence of the Mahayana or the Dharma practice.

In the regular worldly way, without any conceptions of Dharma, love and compassion can be practiced and the practitioner is known as good. Buddha Shakyamuni taught that if you wish to reach enlightenment, you must have loving-kindness and compassion. Without it there is no way to reach enlightenment. So both from the point of view of Dharma or the regular worldly way, compassion and loving-kindness are very special.

The essence
of the
Paramitas
is
*Compassion* and *Loving-kindness*
based upon
Emptiness or True Nature.
This is condensed--
The heart practice of the
Prajnaparamita.

# PART THREE

*The Mind of Enlightenment*

# 5 A Brief History of the Prajnaparamita Books

## The Texts

The understanding of the Prajnaparamita is very profound and very subtle. There are many volumes of Buddha Shakyamuni's teachings on the Prajnaparamita and reading them all takes many years. However, more than studying or learning is involved. A deeper process is implicated.

In Tibet, the Prajnaparamita texts are very popular. In the Buddhist monastic colleges, for example, the Prajnaparamita was studied for eight or nine years and yet there is still more to contemplate.

Buddha taught one hundred million stanzas of teachings of the Prajnaparamita in the god realms, one hundred thousand stanzas in the naga realms and many, many hundreds of stanzas in this human realm.

In the Nalanda Monastery in India twenty huge Prajnaparamita volumes are preserved. They were translated into Tibetan in the Eighth Century during King Trisong Detsen's time. Many of the Prajnaparamita teachings have disappeared, not only in Tibet, but in India and other countries. I think that the Tibetan Cannon is now the most elaborate and complete teaching on the Prajnaparamita existing in this world today. Of course there are many Mahayana Buddhist countries, such as pre-communist China, Japan, Mongolia and Korea. But they don't have as many or as complete Prajnaparamita texts in their language.

During King Trisong Detsen's reign there were many translators, such as the great master Vairochana. King Trisong Detsen himself translated the texts three times with great devotion and deep understanding, copying them in ink of pure gold and precious stones. The gold copy was the first. The second writing is called the Red Prajnaparamita. King Trisong Detsen felt that the gold copy was only a material form and he wished to involve his own body. He hit his nose with his fist, mixed his blood with goat's milk and gold, and made an ink. The Red Prajnaparmita was for his personal use. The third time he cut his hair, burnt it, ground it up, and mixed it with goat milk. This is called the Blue Prajnaparamita. These two, the red and the blue, are famous and kept as royal treasures.

Many Tibetan families then copied the Prajnaparamita text in gold ink. Today Tibetan families of ancient lineage have the Prajnaparamita written in gold or vermilion, keeping it as their family treasure. Most Tibetan families have a copy of the Prajnaparamita.

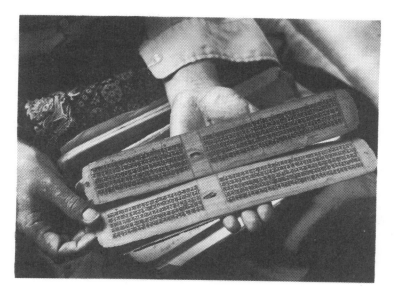

The Prajnaparamita is huge. Each of its twelve volumes has eight or nine thousand stanzas written in gold ink. Special paper is used that is black, very smooth and very thick. Like strong cardboard, it will stand on its own. The letters are decorated and ornamented with precious stones. It's really very heavy, and one must be quite strong to carry even one volume. The pages last for a long time.

If you find a book dating from the eleventh century, it is quite perfect with no damage. Those books that escaped Chinese destruction are perfectly preserved.

Wood block printing came into use around the fifteenth century, making the teachings available to Tibetan families. Regular or vermilion ink was used and many, many editions of the Prajnaparamita as well as Buddha's other teachings became available. "I also carry a very small edition of the Prajnaparmita teaching everywhere I go. It's not gold or silver".

The study of the Prajnaparamita takes a long time. You can hear the words from a master and you can begin to practice. However, the significance of the teachings takes time and maturity. Concentrate upon the teaching and practice as an excellence-for-its-own-sake, without conceit, and concentrate on the wellbeing of others and yourself. Self-liberation will come through the triad of vision, meditation and action. Meditate on Guru Yoga and the radiance of wisdom. Stay in certainty wisdom. When the peak experience of spaciousness dawns, remain in that state.

# 6  *The Essence of the Prajnaparamita is Practice*

The essence of the Prajnaparamita is practice. Although reading, studying and learning produce great benefits, the essence, as Buddha Shakyamuni noted, is the practice.

The Absolute Prajnaparamita is called Primordial Wisdom or the wisdom of enlightened beings. The omniscient state of a Buddha is known as the Absolute Prajnaparamita.

Although we must learn and practice, the Absolute Prajnaparamita is something we all have naturally inherited, and we can therefore achieve it. The Absolute Prajnaparamita is achieved by combining the paramita practices with the practice of Bodhicitta--the beneficial thought, or the mind of enlightenment. We have to work with the Relative Bodhicitta, because the Absolute Bodhicitta is beyond our capacity and wisdom at the present. The relative truth is within our capabilities. Through the Relative Bodhicitta we can attain this Absolute State.

We divide this Prajnaparamita into the relative and absolute. We should start with the relative and then go to the absolute Prajnaparamita. We recognize conscious mood transitions and the availability of joy, playfulness, compassion, loving-kindness and the value of self-governance and empowerment.

## Bodhicitta —The Mind of Enlightenment

Bodhicitta is compassion and loving-kindness. Bodhicitta is a Sanskrit word meaning mind of the Buddha, or enlightenment mind. Bodhicitta is the beneficial thought for all sentient beings, equally and without any expectations.

From the bottom of your heart feel great compassion and loving-kindness for all sentient beings. Feel "from today on, I am going to work for the sentient beings, as much as I can, according to my capabilities and toward increasing my abilities ten times more." That kind of attitude is Bodhicitta.

## Actualizing the Bodhicitta Practice
## (Mind of Enlightenment)

Intention precedes activity. From the bottom of your heart create the intentionality to be of benefit to all sentient beings and respect the environment. Take the beginning steps. Work in that direction. This is called Action Practice, or actualizing the bodhicitta practice. Your intentions are mingling and moving towards the benefit of the earth environment and sentient beings.

Perhaps you are wondering why do we need to help the other sentient beings? We are all interdependent with each other and the earth for our well being.

Every sentient being wants happiness. No one wants suffering or miserable conditions. Everyone hopes for love and peace. Everyone's intention is towards well being. Yet people are not achieving that state all the time. They are not fulfilling their wishes. We should feel great compassion. We should be of assistance, helping them achieve their noble wishes.

Therefore, Bodhicitta purpose is to benefit others. It benefits oneself, too. If we want enlightenment,

Bodhicitta, beneficial thought is definitely the way. Bodhicitta is the way of revealing that absolute state of the Prajnaparamita.

If we don't want enlightenment, then there is nothing to do; this is another question. But Action Practice is for those people who want to reach the enlightenment state and remove old obscurations; who want to work, develop and create their own bodhicitta, their own true compassion.

If we think only of our own benefit, as we have done before, the great result cannot occur. We know this, and it's called selfishness. Even friends don't like selfishness. If even our friends don't like selfishness, it's apparent that we cannot develop realization by being selfish.

By reversing our attitude, not concentrating only on ourselves but paying more attention to other sentient beings, we open our compassion, our hearts. Through this method we achieve our own goals as well as others. Through this mutual aim everyone will feel joy.

# 7   Awakening the Absolute Transcendent Wisdom

We make distinctions in a worldly way between good and bad people. The distinction rests on their compassion for others. There is no sign or color between the good person and the bad person.

By understanding the value of bodhicitta--the thought of enlightenment, a global awareness takes place. When we develop this love and compassion in our heart and mind, we plant the seeds of awakening the Absolute Prajnaparamita State.

Loving-kindness, Compassion, Joyfulness -- all these practices are known as the Relative Prajnaparamita Practices. With these Bodhicitta practices, we should do the other Prajnaparamita Practices. Work and act in a beneficial way through these six practices:

*Generosity*
*Discipline*
*Tolerance*
*Joyful Effort*
*Concentration*
*Wisdom*

## Primordial Wisdom

Together with the six paramitas we do practices called Skillful Means and Aspirations. These are the abilities and primordial wisdom aspects. Even if we don't know too much at the beginning, learning will increase because the potential or seed is within us.

As your ability increases, wisdom removes all obscurations. Through joyful effort your development and realization will grow more and more.

At each level of Bodhicitta or the Prajnaparamita, your ability increases. In this way we can achieve the Five Paths and the Ten Bhumis. The Five Paths and the Ten

Bhumis are the inner realization states. These are not external existents. The Five Paths and the Ten Bhumis are the inner measurement of the realization state.

## The Five Paths

### 1. The Accumulation Path

The first path is called the Accumulation Path. At this time your virtuous activity and accumulation activities or energies are growing.

### 2. The Application Path

The second stage is called the Application Path and this is the result of the Accumulation Path. When you reach this stage you won't have too much trouble with clinging and attachments to things. You will also have strong powers and abilities.

In the post meditative state, you will see everything as a reflection, like the moon on the water. You will not feel too many distractions towards objects. Phenomena appear as in a mirage. Such realization gives more abilities and freedom than in the past.

### 3. The Seeing Path

The Third Path is called the Seeing Path, which is the pith understanding of the second path, the Application

Path. This is the real seeing. Until now your meditation or seeing is still mingled with imagination or theory—that is relative truth. Now in the Seeing Path, you see the true nature face to face, with your own clear awareness.

*In this third path, the Seeing Path,*
*you see or realize the Absolute Prajnaparamita*
*perfectly,*
*without any obscuration or blockage.*
*You really see innerly.*
*Therefore, this stage is known as the Seeing Path.*
*Not imagining or guessing,*
*nor theoretically understanding,*
*but seeing the perfection of insight and meaning.*
*The Seeing Path.*

*When you reach this stage,*
*ability is higher and stronger*
*than the second path.*

*Your ability is very strong,*
*benefiting the sentient beings*
*and the earth environment.*

*At the same time you accomplish much.*
*Everything is quite free.*
*You control the fears of death and rebirth.*
*Also, you control many obstacles*
*such as sickness.*

*You can do as you want.*
*Your plans are well scheduled,*
*well ordered,*
*well established.*

*You can perform all activities.*
*This stage is also called the Fearlessness Stage.*
*When you reach this third stage,*
*you are free from fears*
*such as getting old,*
*sickness,*
*death--*
*since the subtle profound nature of*
*emptiness is realized.*

*You are self-liberated*
*and at the same time you have great joy*
*and happiness.*

This is the start of the great joy state. Until now your happiness has always been mingled with emotion and impermanence. Joy had been experienced one day, the next day was different and the next day emotions changed again. Now this first bhumi is called the joyful path.

**The First Bhumi is called the State of Extreme Joy.**

"Here standing
on the stage of
Extreme Joy
of enlightening beings
one is filled with extreme joy
filled with calm
filled with happiness
filled with ebullience,
filled with exaltation
filled with delight,
greatly invigorated,
most uncontentious,
most harmless,
and free from anger."

*The Flower Ornament Scripture: The Avatamsaka Sutra: Volume 11, Shambhala Publications.*

## 4. *The Meditation Path*

The fourth path is called the Meditation Path. This is a continuation of the third path, the Seeing Path Practice. There is no special effort. It is spontaneous, the perfection of insight in a mingling of the post meditation state and the meditation state into one single state, so that there is no difference. All are one natural state. This is called the Ultimate State of the meditation.

## 5. *Absolute Prajnaparamita State*

Of course, by this time
your meditation ability
your realization
your ability
your joy
your understanding and wisdom grow more and more
till the ultimate state which is called
*"Path Of No More Studying"*.
That State is also known as Budhhahood.

Another name for the no more studying state is the Absolute Prajnaparamita State.

There is no more to learn
no more to know --
you have discovered all in that state.

This state has many different synonyms:
Perfect Enlightenment State,
Buddhahood,
Perfectly Discovered Prajnaparamita State,
Absolute Prajnaparamita.
In the teachings there are many different names
but this is the ultimate state of the true nature
or Enlightenment.

## ENLIGHTENMENT

Therefore, it is very important for us to start with good practice, practice on loving-kindness and compassion. When you start with the seed of good love or true compassion, the result will be perfect.

In the mundane way too, when we have good seeds and good conditions, and we plant in good soil, we definitely get good results. If we start with insufficient causes and conditions, if we plant in poor soil and don't take the proper care, we won't get good results. Everything follows the system we call cause and effect. Good cause (Loving-kindness, Compassion and Wisdom) definitely brings good results—Enlightenment or the Absolute Prajnaparamita State.

*Therefore,
it is very important
for us to start with good practice,
practice on Loving-kindness and
Compassion.*

*When you start
with the seed of good love or true
compassion,
the result will be perfect.*

# 8 Two Accumulation Practices

In Mahayana texts this practice is known as Two Accumulation Practices. The first is called The Accumulation Merit Practice, and the second is called the Wisdom Merit Practice. These two merits are important in order to achieve enlightenment and are combined with the bodhicitta (loving-kindness and compassion).

## 1. The Accumulation Merit Practice

What is the difference between the two merits? The Accumulation Merit is Relative Truth Practice, that

is doing all the beneficial activities, such as generosity, self-discipline, tolerance or patience, joyful effort, concentration, etc..

## 2. The Wisdom Merit Practice

The Wisdom Merit is beyond any activity by body, speech, or mind. Maintain mind in the absolute state of the Prajnaparamita. At this moment we may not realize the absolute Prajnparamita state, but we can definitely feel, and roughly know the absolute Prajnaparamita when we meditate. This dynamic is the process of unfolding mind becoming increasingly aware of itself as a self-organizing principle. The meditation practice is known then as the Wisdom Merit Meditation Practice. During the post meditation state, whatever activities are performed by compassion and loving-kindness are known as Accumulation Practice.

By these two practices, the result achieved will be in Buddhahood timing -- the two Kayas. You may be familiar with that terminology, Dharmakaya and Rupakaya.

# 9  Dharmakaya and Rupakaya

Dharmakaya is the result of the meditation practices or the wisdom practice. Rupakaya is the result of accumulation practice.

Now, our compassion and loving-kindness may be very limited. However, this limited compassion and loving-kindness can grow to limitless stages.

Therefore, we should not feel discouraged, tired or lazy. We should start in a simple or limited way. We needn't say, "Oh this is too small, why did I bother?" That kind of attitude is not right. We should start from the minimal way. Go by your own abilities. Do what you can do and let it develop through small steps.

This is how we should practice. Take small steps each time and practice diligently with joyful effort. Don't ignore even the small activities. Do those activities with good intentions and dedicate the merit from them to all sentient beings.

This is the Prajnaparamita practice through which we can reach the Absolute Prajnaparamita State. Mingle the Prajnaparamita practice with daily activities. Feel no separation between the two -- the practice time and the mundane time of ordinary activities. Otherwise you will not be able to transform everything into the Prajnaparamita practice.

Start this moment and mingle every activity with the Prajnaparmita, that is, with love and compassion and bodhicitta. When we are able to mingle bodhicitta, love, and compassion with all our activities during the daytime, spontaneously we will also be able to mingle our bodhicitta with our dream activity. We then have the ability to mingle all activities -- both day and night into the bodhicitta or Prajnaparamita State.

This will help when we are dying. At the moment of our death, we can transform our death. This is also part of the Prajnaparamita practices. It is not that something solid and terrible is happening. We will see it as display or mirage or illusion. If we can do that, then after death, (which in Buddhism is called the bardo state, or the intermediate state), we can transform into the Prajnaparamita state. Throughout your lifetime you will be able to mingle all in the Prajnaparamita state. You will then perceive everything as a mirage or a reflection of the moon in the water. Then you do not have too many  serious problems or hardships through those transitions and different states.

In the Vajrayana, the Prajnaparamita is also practiced in many different ways, such as visualizing the deity and reciting mantra. Such learning skills are quite ancient. Concentration, one-pointing of mind, creative imagery and the art of dreaming, creative will, energy exchange, the honoring of earth and nature, and calmness are necessary for healing arts and transformative skills. This is also part of the practice on the Prajnaparamita.

# AFTERWORD

## *The Sutra of the Heart of Transcendant Knowledge*

# The Sutra of the Heart
# of Transcendant Knowledge

"Thus have I heard. Once the Blessed One was dwelling in Rajagrha at Vulture Peak mountain, together with a great gathering of the sangha of monks and a great gathering of the sangha of bodhisattvas. At that time the Blessed One entered the samadhi that expresses the dharma called *"profound illumination,"* and at the same time noble Avalokitesvara, the bodhisattva mahasattva, while practicing the profound prajnaparamita, saw in this way: he saw the five skandhas to be empty of nature.

Then, through the power of the Buddha, venerable Sariputra said to noble Avalokitesvara, the bodhisattva mahasattva, "How should a son or daughter of noble family train, who wishes to practice the profound prajnaparamita?"

Addressed in this way, noble Avalokitesvara, the bodhisattva mahasattva, said to venerable Sariputra, "O Sariputra, a son or daughter of noble family who wishes to practice the profound prajnaparamita should see in this way: seeing the five skandhas to be empty of nature. Form is emptiness; emptiness also is form. Emptiness is no other than form; form is no other than emptiness. In the same way, feeling, perception, formation and consciousness are emptiness. Thus, Sariputra, all dharmas are emptiness. There are no characteristics. There is no birth and no cessation. There is no impurity and no purity. There is no decrease and no increase. Therefore, Sariputra, in emptiness, there is no form, no feeling, no perception, no formation, no consciousness; no eye, no ear, no nose, no tongue, no body, no mind; no appearance, no sound, no smell, no taste, no touch, no dharmas; no eye dhatu up to no mind dhatu, no dhatu of dharmas, no mind consciousness dhatu; no ignorance, no end of ignorance up to no old age and death, no end of old age and death; no suffering, no origin of suffering, no cessation of suffering, no path, no wisdom, no attainment, and no nonattainment. Therefore, Sariputra, since the bodhisattvas have no attainment, they abide by means of prajnaparamita. Since there is no obscuration of mind, there is no fear. They transcend falsity and attain complete nirvana.   All the buddhas of the three times, by means of prajnaparamita, fully awaken to unsurpassable, true, complete enlightenment. Therefore, the great mantra of prajnaparamita, the mantra of great insight, the unsurpassed mantra, the unequaled mantra, the mantra that calms all suffering should be known as truth, since there is no deception. The prajnaparamita mantra is said in this way:

**Tayatha Om Gate Gate Paragate Parasamgate Bodhi Svaha**

Thus Sariputra, the bodhisattva mahasattva should train in the profound prajnaparamita.

Then the Blessed One arose from that samadhi and praised noble Avalokitesvara, the bodhisattva mahasattva, saying, "Good, good, O son of noble family; thus it is, O son of noble family, thus it is. One should practice the profound prajnaparamita just as you have taught and all the tathagatas will rejoice.

When the Blessed One had said this, venerable Sariputra and noble Avalokitesvara, the bodhisattva mahasattva, that whole assembly and the world with its gods, humans, asuras, and gandharvas rejoiced and praised the words of the Blessed One."

*Lotsawa bhiksu Rinchen De translated this text into Tibetan with the Indian pandita Vimalamitra. It was edited by the great editor-lotsawas Gelo, Namkha, and others. This Tibetan text was copied from the fresco in Gegye Chemaling at the glorious Samye vihara. It has been translated into English by the Nalanda Translation Committee, with reference to several Sanskit editions.*

# FOR THE SARNATH PROJECT

## PRAJNAPARAMITA:
### The Heart Of Transcendent Wisdom

*written by*
The Ven. Khenpo Palden Sherab Rinpoche
*translated by*
The Ven. Khenpo Tsewang Dongyal Rinpoche

A New Nyingma Text
Special Limited, Numbered Hardcover Edition
Personally inscribed to you by the Khen Rinpoche
Gold embossed with Full Color photographs
Available Summer 1992

*" A rare treasure -- a family heirloom "*

The first 100 copies that are printed
will be a special collector's edition -- individually
numbered and inscribed personally by
Khenpo Palden to you with his official seal.
These will be allocated on a first come first served basis.

Please send all inquiries to:
*Sky Dancer Press*
P.O. Box 1830
Boca Raton, Florida 33429

We will be most happy to hear from you.

*Sky Dancer Press*
*is happy to announce the forthcoming books:*

# The Great Completion: Dzog Chen

The Ven. Khenpo Palden Sherab Rinpoche's Teachings

Translated by
The Ven. Khenpo Tsewang Dongyal Rinpoche

---

**Sky Dancer Yeshey Tshogyal:**
**Lady of the Lake**
by
The Ven. Khenpo Palden Sherab Rinpoche

translated by
The Ven. Khenpo Tsewang Dongyal Rinpoche